PHILOSOPHY IN
40 IDEAS

The School of Life

Contents

Introduction

Philosophy is a deeply unpopular subject that almost no one knows anything much about. The average school doesn't teach it, the average adult doesn't understand it – and the whole subject can seem scary, strange and not very necessary.

All of this is a huge pity, because philosophy has a lot to say to everyone at any age. It might be the most important subject you'll never be asked to study. We want to start opening the door by taking you on a tour of the history of philosophy's greatest ideas.

The word 'philosophy' itself starts to tell us why the subject matters. It's originally a word from Ancient Greek. The first part – *philo* – means love. The second part, *sophia*, means wisdom. So philo-sophy means, quite literally, 'the love of wisdom'.

Philosophy is one of the great ways in which human beings can deal with the difficulties of life. It's a storehouse of the best and richest ideas about confronting our tricky moments. Right at the beginning of its life, philosophy used to be done outdoors, in the public square, by ordinary people. That's how one of the great early philosophers, Socrates, did it. Socrates lived in Athens more than two thousand years ago. He wore long robes (like everyone else in those days); he had a long beard, and he liked to walk about the city and meet his friends and ask them questions about what they were excited or worried or puzzled about. His idea was that often people don't know why they have the thoughts and feelings they do. Socrates used philosophy to help us understand ourselves better. Socrates was very keen on the word 'why'. He was always asking people tricky 'why' questions: why are you friends with this person; why don't you like so-and so? He wasn't being mean or awkward. He really wanted to have an interesting discussion. He wanted to be people's thinking friend.

Since Socrates's time, philosophy has become a lot less public, friendly and useful. It's often done in universities by people with no interest in improving the world right now.

Fortunately, philosophy is now back on the public agenda and we can all benefit from its fruits. You too can be a bit like Socrates and be your own thinking friend by asking yourself the biggest questions. Welcome to the conversation.

Know yourself

SOCRATES, the earliest and greatest of Western philosophers, summed up the purpose of philosophy in one simple phrase: 'know yourself'. In giving this motto such importance in his thought, Socrates was alluding to a big problem with being human: we normally don't know ourselves very well, although, fatefully, we might feel as if we do. The spotlight of consciousness usually only shines on a small part of what is really going on inside us. We are governed by forces we rarely pay attention to: envy, disavowed anger, buried hurt, ideas from childhood that have come to frame our outlook but that we hardly realise we possess. The consequences of this ignorance are typically disastrous. As an antidote, Socrates advocated the regular, careful examination of our minds. He recommended systematically asking ourselves, ideally in the company of a patient and thoughtful friend, questions like: what are my priorities? What do I really fear? What do I truly want? Investigating and interpreting our thoughts and feelings was, and remains, the essence of what it means to be a philosopher.

Philo-sophia

IN ANCIENT GREEK, *philo* means love, *sophia* wisdom. Quite literally, a philosopher is someone with an unusually powerful love of wisdom. The concept of wisdom can sound abstract and lofty, but it isn't. We can and should all strive to be a little wiser. The wise are, first and foremost, realistic about how challenging many things can be. They are fully conscious of the complexities entailed in any project. They rarely expect anything to be wholly easy or to go entirely well. As a result, they are unusually alive to moments of calm and beauty – even extremely modest ones. The wise know that all human beings, themselves included, are never far from folly. Aware that at least half of life is irrational, they try – wherever possible – to budget for madness, and are slow to panic when it rears its head. The wise know how to laugh at the constant collisions between the noble way they would like things to be, and the demented way they often turn out.

Eudaimonia

THIS IS AN ANCIENT GREEK WORD, normally translated as 'fulfilment', particularly emphasised by the philosopher Aristotle. It deserves wider currency because it corrects the shortfalls in one of the most central terms in our contemporary idiom: happiness. The Ancient Greeks resolutely did not believe that the purpose of life was to be happy; they proposed that it was to be *fulfilled*. What distinguishes *happiness* from fulfilment is pain. It is eminently possible to be fulfilled and, at the same time, under pressure, suffering physically or mentally, overburdened and in a tetchy mood. Many of life's most worthwhile projects will, at points, be quite at odds with contentment, but may be worth pursuing nevertheless. Henceforth, we shouldn't try to be happy; we should accept the greater realism, ambition and patience that accompanies the quest for *eudaimonia*.

Democracy

DEMOCRACY IS A BEAUTIFUL IDEA: everyone's vote is equal, whatever their income or education. It feels wicked to say anything against it. Yet democracy is obviously a touch unreasonable – and the Greek philosophers knew it. Plato said so most clearly in *The Republic*: it is impossible that every person's view can be equally astute. A democratic vote is like the captain of a ship having to consult every passenger about the best course to chart through an approaching storm. For admirable reasons, we are committed to a political system that is problematic. According to Plato, the solution should be intense universal education to foster wisdom in everyone. We cannot allow everyone to vote until everyone has learnt to think. Till then, we need to laugh at the tragi-comic nature of our predicament. There will be a lot of erratic choices. The Ancient Greek philosophers – whom we mistakenly believe all loved democracy – had a clear-eyed view of the many problems that might crop up. After all, they invented the word 'demagogue' to describe a political leader who, in a democracy, sweeps into power by collecting votes through appeals to the lower passions rather than to higher reason.

Eros and philia

VERY EARLY ON, GREEK PHILOSOPHY TWIGGED that love is not really one thing but a cluster of very different emotions and attitudes that we should carefully distinguish between. Having an array of words for love can spare us the perils of a simple-minded sense that we are no longer 'in love' when we've merely moved onto a different, but still authentically real, phase of love. The Greeks anointed the powerful physical feelings we often experience at the start of a relationship with the word *eros*. But they knew that love is not necessarily over when this sexual intensity wanes, as it almost always does. It can evolve into another sort of love, which they beautifully captured with the word *philia*. This is normally translated as 'friendship', although the Greek word is far warmer, more loyal and more touching; one might be willing to die for *philia*. Aristotle recommended that we outgrow *eros* in youth, and then base our relationships – especially our marriages – on *philia* instead. The word adds an important nuance to our understanding of a viable union. It allows us to see that we may still love even when we are in a phase that our own blunter vocabulary fails to recognise.

*'What need is there to weep over
parts of life? The whole of it calls for tears'*

THE ROMAN PHILOSOPHER SENECA used to comfort his friends – and himself – with this darkly humorous remark. It gets to the heart of Stoicism, the school of philosophy that Seneca helped to found and that dominated the West for 200 years. We become weepy and furious, says Stoicism, not simply because our plans have failed, but because they have failed and we strongly expected them not to. Therefore, thought Seneca, the task of philosophy is to disappoint us gently before life has a chance to do so violently. The less we expect, the less we will suffer. Through the help of a consoling pessimism, we should strive to turn our rage and tears into that far less volatile compound: sadness. Seneca was not trying to depress us, just to spare us the kind of hope that, when it fails, inspires bitterness and intemperate shouting.

Peccatum originale

IN THE LATE 4TH CENTURY, as the immense Roman Empire was collapsing, the leading philosopher of the age, St Augustine, became interested in possible explanations for the tragic disorder of the human world. One central idea he developed was what he legendarily termed *peccatum originale*: original sin. Augustine proposed that human nature is inherently damaged and tainted because, in the Garden of Eden, the mother of all people, Eve, sinned against God by eating an apple from the Tree of Knowledge. Her guilt was then passed down to her descendants and now all earthly human endeavours are bound to fail because they are the work of a corrupt and faulty human spirit. This odd idea might not be literally true, of course. However, as a metaphor for why the world is in a mess, it has a beguiling poetic truth, as relevant to atheists as to believers. We should not expect too much from the human race, Augustine implies; we've been somewhat doomed from the outset. That can be a redemptive thought to keep in mind.

MONTAIGNE 1533 1592

'Kings and philosophers shit, and so do ladies'

THE BLUNT PHRASE APPEARS in an essay by the 16th-century French philosopher, Michel de Montaigne. Montaigne wasn't being mean. His point was kindly: he wanted us to feel closer to (and less intimidated by) people whose lives might seem impressive and very far from our own. He could have added: in secret, these people also feel inadequate, fear rejection and mess up their sex lives. We could update his examples to speak of CEOs, entrepreneurs, and the over-achievers we went to college with. Montaigne was attempting to free us from lack of confidence and shyness, born from an exaggerated sense of the differences between ourselves and mighty others. At moments of panic, before an important speech or a much-anticipated date, we should run Montaigne's phrase through our febrile, underconfident minds and remind ourselves that no one, however outwardly poised, is more than a few hours away from a poignantly modest and vulnerable moment.

'All our unhappiness comes from our inability to sit alone in our room'

THIS ASSERTION, by the 17th-century French philosopher Blaise Pascal, is obviously not literally true. However, like all good philosophical aphorisms, it pointedly exaggerates an important idea in order to bring home a general insight. We are tempted to leave 'our room' and crave excitements that too often turn out badly; we meddle in the lives of others but fail to help them; we seek fame and end up being misunderstood by large numbers of people we don't know. 'Sitting alone' doesn't mean literally perching on our bed but, rather, staying undistracted with ourselves – appreciating small pleasures; examining the contents of our own minds; allowing the quieter parts of our psyches to emerge; thinking before we act. It is a poignant phrase because the louder voices in our culture constantly speak in the opposite direction. They goad us to get out more, to grow more agitated, to seek more drama and to spend less time in thoughtful reveries, gazing out of the window at the clouds passing high above. With Pascal's encouragement, we should learn to become better friends to ourselves.

Sub specie aeternitatis

TRANSLATED FROM THE LATIN, this means 'under the aspect of eternity'. This memorable phrase comes from the *Ethics*, published in 1677 by the Dutch philosopher Baruch Spinoza. For Spinoza, the task of philosophy is to teach us to look at things, especially our own suffering and disappointment, 'under the aspect of eternity'; that is, as though we were gazing down at the Earth from very far away or from a different star (Spinoza's outlook was much indebted to Galileo). From this lofty perspective, the incidents that trouble us no longer have to seem so shocking or so large. What is a divorce or a sacking when contemplated from the lunar surface? What is a rejection in love judged against the Earth's 4.5-billion-year history? Our nature means that we will always tend to exaggerate the here and now, but our reasoned intelligence gives us access to a unique alternative perspective. We can participate in what Spinoza called 'eternal totality' and can cease railing against the status quo, instead submitting to the flow of events with clear-eyed serenity.

Machiavellianism

NICCOLO MACHIAVELLI was a 16th-century Florentine political philosopher whose thought pivots around a central, uncomfortable observation: that the wicked tend to win. They do so because they have a huge advantage over the good: they are willing to act with the darkest ingenuity and cunning to further their cause. Machiavelli's goal – set out most famously in his book, *The Prince* – was to teach good people to behave with the same forcefulness as the bad. In his view, the admirable prince (and today we might add the CEO, political activist or thinker) should learn every lesson from the slickest, most devious operators. They should know how to scare and intimidate, cajole and bully, entrap and beguile. If we care about wisdom, kindness, seriousness and virtue, but only ever act wisely, kindly, seriously and virtuously, we will get nowhere. We may sometimes have to act in a Machiavellian way, not because we are ourselves wicked, but because getting anything done in a rough world demands that we act for a time with all the single-minded coldness of baddies.

*Aus so krummem Holze, als woraus
der Mensch gemacht ist, kann nichts ganz
Gerades gezimmert werden.*

THIS LONG AND SLIGHTLY DAUNTING GERMAN phrase is also hugely arresting and redemptive, and central to the spirit of Western philosophy: 'Out of the crooked timber of humanity, no straight thing was ever made.' So wrote the 18th-century German philosopher Immanuel Kant, who urged us to recognise that everything that human beings do will be slightly wonky, because we are as much creatures of passion and erroneous instinct as of reason and noble intelligence. The wise accept this dark reality head on and so do not expect perfection. When designing governments, they do not presume that rationality will triumph; they assume that error and folly will try to have their way, and create structures to contain them. When they marry, with comparable realism, they never expect that one person can be everything to them, and so do not harangue their partner when they turn out not to be. An acceptance of our crooked nature is not dispiriting; it is the birth of generosity and dark good humour. And, Kant added, crooked beams can make for beautiful floors in the hands of a talented carpenter.

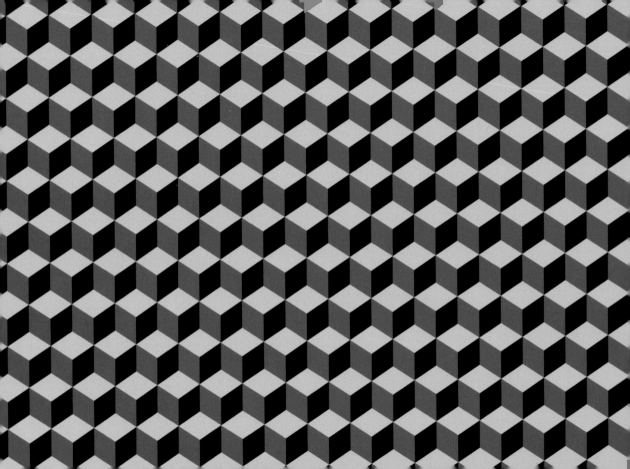

The Hegelian dialectic of history

IN HIS LECTURES ON THE PHILOSOPHY OF WORLD HISTORY, published in 1830, the German philosopher Georg Wilhelm Friedrich Hegel proposed that history moves forward in what he termed a dialectical way. A dialectic is a philosophical term for an argument made up of three parts: a thesis, an antithesis and a synthesis. Both the thesis and the antithesis contain parts of the truth, but are exaggerations and distortions of it, so they need to clash and interact until their best elements find resolution in a synthesis. Hegel proposed that the world makes progress only by lurching from one extreme to another and generally requires three moves before the right balance on any issue can be found. He reminds us that big overreactions are eminently compatible with events broadly moving forward in the right direction. The dark moments of history aren't the end; they are a challenging, but (in some ways) necessary, part of an antithesis that will eventually locate a wiser point of synthesis. With Hegel in mind, we must strive to be patient with the zigzag course of events.

'God is dead'

THIS LEGENDARY STATEMENT, which heralds the arrival of the secular age in Western history, appears in Friedrich Nietzsche's book of 1882, *The Gay Science*. It can sound triumphant, but Nietzsche didn't mean it that way. He felt that the death of God was going to be very difficult for humanity. He feared that we would too quickly reject many good things that religion had, at its best, promoted. He predicted a loss of emphasis on community, charity and compassion; a decline in a sense of awe; and a new faith in what he thought were two unreliable sources of meaning: romantic love and professional success. Nietzsche's hope wasn't to get rid of religion altogether; it was to replace it with a better sort of religion, one based on art, music and philosophy – a creed whose heroes would be the Stoic philosophers, Montaigne, Goethe and Wagner. God might have died, said Nietzsche, but we would only create a good godless world if we kept in mind why we had invented him in the first place and appreciated how many of those reasons remained.

The Sublime

THE CONCEPT OF THE SUBLIME refers to an experience of vastness (of space, age or time) beyond calculation or comprehension – a sense of awe that we might feel before an ocean, a glacier, the Earth from a plane, or a starry sky. Its best early definition came from Edmund Burke's book *A Philosophical Enquiry into the Origin of Our Ideas of the Sublime and Beautiful,* published in 1757. In the presence of the Sublime, Burke argued, we are made to feel desperately small. In most of life, a sense of our smallness is experienced as a humiliation (when it happens, for example, at the hands of a professional enemy or a waiter). But the impression of smallness that unfolds in the presence of the Sublime has an uplifting and profoundly redemptive effect. We are granted an impression of our complete nullity and insignificance in a grander scheme, which relieves us of an often-oppressive sense of the seriousness of our ambitions and desires. The Sublime grants us a perspective from which our own concerns seem mercifully irrelevant.

The Wealth of Nations

THIS IS POSSIBLY THE MOST INFLUENTIAL philosophy book of the 18th century, published by Adam Smith in 1776. In it, Smith sought to show how nations increase their productivity. They do so, he said, through the 'division of labour'. When workers cease to be generalists and specialise instead, the overall output of a nation rises exponentially. Specialisation makes huge economic sense but, as Smith knew, it can create profound private sorrows. As his heirs, we have all become very small cogs in gargantuan machines whose overall purpose we are liable to lose sight of day to day. It is painfully common to wonder what one's job might be 'for'. It will have a purpose, knew Smith, but this purpose may not be in any way tangible for an individual worker. To overcome this feeling of meaninglessness, Smith proposed that we learn the art of storytelling, so as to reveal the real but usually hidden grandeur of every specialised worker's seemingly small contribution to a bigger, but nowadays less identifiable, narrative.

Existential Angst

WE ARE FREQUENTLY THROWN into anxiety by our need to make a choice between options, in situations where we lack the necessary information and cannot be certain of the future. We are then in a condition known as Existential Angst. At such moments, the real choice is almost never between error and happiness but between varieties of suffering. This is the wisdom of the early 19th-century Danish philosopher Søren Kierkegaard, summed up in a playful, but bleakly realistic and exasperated, outburst in his masterpiece, *Either/Or:* 'Hang yourself, you will regret it; do not hang yourself, and you will regret that too; hang yourself or don't hang yourself, you'll regret it either way; whether you hang yourself or do not hang yourself, you will regret both. This, gentlemen, is the essence of all philosophy.' We deserve pity; we will make disastrous decisions, but we can – says Kierkegaard – be consoled by a bitter truth: we have no better options, for the conditions of existence are intrinsically rather than accidentally frustrating. There is, curiously, a relief to be found in the knowledge of the inevitability of suffering, which is what makes Kierkegaard fun, or at least consoling, to read. In the end, it is not darkness that dooms us, but the wrong sort of hope.

Bad faith

THE 20TH-CENTURY FRENCH PHILOSOPHER Jean-Paul Sartre gave a term to the way we often deny that we are free and have options to change our lives; he called it 'bad faith'. Because change is hard, we have a tendency to tell ourselves that things have to be a certain way, that we have to do a particular kind of work or live with a specific person or make our home in a given place. Sartre felt that married people and office workers were particularly prone to living in 'bad faith'. They might pretend to themselves that they had to endure a tricky spouse or an unimaginative clerical position when they were in fact always free to leave. Realising one's freedom in Sartre's sense should not be confused with an idea, found in certain works of American self-help, that we're all free to be or do more or less anything great without suffering or sacrifice. Sartre is far gloomier and more tragic than this. He merely wants to point out that we have many more options than we normally believe – even if in some cases the leading option (which Sartre defended vigorously) might be to become a tramp and wander the open roads of the Earth in a penniless, outcast yet liberated state.

The Myth of Sisyphus

THIS WAS THE TITLE OF one of the most widely read books of 20th-century philosophy, published by Albert Camus in 1942. It has a very famous first sentence: 'There is but one truly serious philosophical problem and that is suicide.' The reason for this stark claim is, in Camus's eyes, because as soon as we start to think seriously, as philosophers will, we stand to see that life has no intrinsic meaning – and therefore we will be compelled to wonder why we even bother to exist. In many ways, says Camus, we are like Sisyphus, the Greek figure ordered by the gods to roll a boulder up a mountain and watch it fall back down again in perpetuity. Camus argues that we have to acknowledge the absurd background to existence but then triumph over the constant possibility of hopelessness. In his famous formulation: 'We must imagine Sisyphus *happy*.' As part of this effort at re-enchantment, Camus tries to remind himself and us of the many reasons why life can be worth enduring. He writes with exceptional charm about relationships, nature, the beach, holidays, football and summer evenings – some of the ingredients that best protect us against a haunting background sense of meaninglessness.

Being and Time

IN THE COMPETITIVE HISTORY of incomprehensible German philosophers, Martin Heidegger must be counted as the overall victor. Nothing quite rivals the dense yet brilliant prose of his masterpiece *Being and Time* (1927). In it, Heidegger argues that in our day-to-day lives we aren't properly in touch with the sheer mystery of life, or of what he calls (from the title) 'das Sein' or 'Being'. It's only at a few odd times – perhaps late at night or on a walk in nature – that we come up against the uncanny strangeness of everything and wonder why things exist as they do: why we are here rather than there; why the world is like this; why that tree or this house are the way they are. We are reminded to wonder – and philosophise. To capture these rare moments when the normal state of things wobbles a little, Heidegger talks, with capital letters, of the Mystery of Being. His entire philosophy is devoted to getting us to appreciate, and respond appropriately to, the wondrous strangeness of existence.

The Vinegar-Tasters

A FAVOURITE SUBJECT FOR ASIAN ARTISTS for many centuries was a depiction of the three founding figures of Eastern philosophy – Confucius, Buddha and Lao Tzu – standing together and each reacting in a characteristic way to the taste of vinegar. Confucius, who speaks of the respect we should have for tradition and our elders, sees vinegar as a miserable 'descendant' of its noble 'ancestor': wine. This is logical, because for Confucius, ancestors are typically superior to those who come after. For his part, the Buddha hates the taste and turns away from it in sadness. For him, the world is a vale of bitter tears and salvation comes only from disengaging from it as much as possible. But the last figure, Lao Tzu, the founder of Daoism, is pleased. Not because he likes the taste of vinegar particularly, but because he always greets existence with benevolent curiosity. Three attitudes to the world in one image. We're not being asked to choose, simply selectively to experience the distinctive wisdom of each position.

Zhōng (CHINESE): *Loyalty*

AT THE CORE OF CONFUCIANISM is an emphasis on loyalty – in part because Confucius knew how tempting it is to use people in an instrumental way and drop them as soon as they have ceased to be of service to us. But when we practise the virtue of *zhōng*, we're invited to interpret people's less admirable behaviour far more generously. If they can no longer give us things and may be tricky or boring, we should imagine that this is not the result of wickedness but of suffering, illness or anxiety. The loyal are those who offer explanations for others' misdeeds that take extenuating circumstances into account. Loyalty means generating a picture of who other people are that renders them more than simply mean, mad or repulsive. Confucius reminds us that the need for loyalty is unlikely to end up being one-sided; we will all – especially as we age – be powerfully in need of the loyalty of others.

The Five Virtues

MODERN CULTURE places huge emphasis on training to be physically fit. Confucius emphasised the importance of training to be morally good. This sounds strange, reminding us of how much our culture overlooks the pursuit of ethical development. Confucius identified five central virtues that make us good: compassion (*ren*), ritual propriety (*li*), justice (*yi*), knowledge (*zhi*) and integrity (*xin*). Crucially, Confucius felt that these five had to be worked on over a whole lifetime. He told his followers: 'At fifteen, I had my mind bent on intellectual learning. At thirty, I was busy and practical. At forty, I had no doubts. At fifty, I started to learn. At sixty, my ear was an obedient organ for the reception of truth. At seventy, I had learnt to follow the five virtues.' In other words, training to be good takes a lot of time. No wonder Confucius revered old people; their skin might not be as supple or their faces as pretty, but – he argued – they stand a slightly higher chance of having learnt to be a little more virtuous than the young and less experienced.

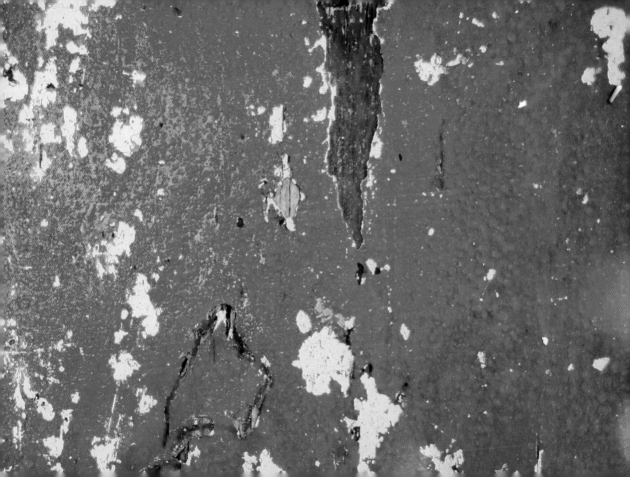

The life of Confucius

CONFUCIANISM HAS COME TO US in a series of anecdotes about the character and way of life of Confucius himself. We aren't asked to read lectures by Confucius about how we should live; we're invited to see how Confucius himself behaved at small and large moments – and then to be inspired by his example. One of the most famous stories, found in the *Analects*, the central book of Confucianism, highlights the importance of putting people before possessions (which, in his day, included animals): 'When the stables were burnt down, on returning from court, Confucius said, "Was anyone hurt?" He did not ask about the horses' (for horses, read Maseratis). To be a follower of Confucius means constantly asking oneself: what would Confucius do now? The philosopher is – above all else – a role model. This is an unexpected but fruitful way of doing philosophy, because we tend not to learn decent behaviour in abstract ways; we have to see goodness enacted in the lives of others before we start to model it ourselves. Confucius, who lived in north-eastern China in the 6th century BCE, emerges as an inspiring, kindly and charming role model with a surprising amount to offer our times.

Life is suffering

THE FIRST AND CENTRAL 'NOBLE TRUTH' of the Buddha is that life is unavoidably about suffering. The Buddha continually seeks to adjust our expectations so we will know what awaits us: sex will disappoint us, youth will disappear, money won't spare us pain. For the Buddha, the wise person should take care to grow completely at home with the ordinary shambles of existence. They should understand that they are living on a dunghill. When baseness and malice rear their heads, as they will, it should be against a backdrop of fully vanquished hope, so there will be no sense of having been unfairly let down or having had one's credulity betrayed. That said, the Buddha was often surprisingly cheerful and generally sported an inviting, warm smile. This was because anything nice, sweet or amusing that came his way was immediately experienced as a bonus; a deeply gratifying addition to his original bleak premises. By keeping the dark backdrop of life always in mind, he sharpened his appreciation of whatever stood out against it. He teaches us the art of cheerful despair.

Mettā (PALI):
Benevolence

IN THE INDIAN LANGUAGE OF PALI, *mettā* means benevolence, kindness or tenderness. It is one of the most important ideas in Buddhism. Buddhism recommends a daily ritual meditation (known as *mettā bhāvāna*) to foster this attitude. The meditation begins with a call to think carefully every morning of an individual with whom one tends to get irritated or to whom one feels aggressive or cold and – in place of one's normal hostile impulses – to rehearse kindly messages like 'I hope you will find peace' or 'I wish you to be free from suffering'. This practice can be extended outwards ultimately to include pretty much everyone on Earth. The background assumption is that, with the right goad, our feelings towards people are not fixed and unalterable, but open to deliberate change and improvement. Compassion is a learnable skill, and we need to direct it as much towards those we are tempted to dismiss and detest as to those we love.

Guanyin

GUANYIN IS A SAINTLY FEMALE in East Asian Buddhism strongly associated with mercy, compassion and kindness. She occupies a similar role within Buddhism as the Virgin Mary within Catholicism. There are shrines and temples to her all over China; a 108-metre statue of her in the province of Hainan is the fourth-largest statue in the world. Guanyin's popularity speaks of the extent to which the needs of childhood endure within us. She is, in the noblest sense, 'mummy'. Across China, adults allow themselves to be weak in her presence. Her gaze has a habit of making people cry – for the moment one breaks down isn't so much when things are hard as when one finally encounters kindness and a chance to admit to sorrows one has been harbouring in silence for too long. Guanyin doesn't judge. She understands that you are tired, that you have been betrayed, that things aren't easy, that you are fed up. She has a measure of the difficulties involved in trying to lead a remotely adequate adult life.

Wu Wei (CHINESE):
Not making an effort

WU WEI is a term at the heart of the philosophy of Daoism. It is first described in the *Tao Te Ching*, written by the sage Lao Tzu in the 6th century BCE. *Wu wei* means 'not making an effort', or going with the flow, but does not in any way imply laziness or sloth. It suggests an intentional surrender of the will based on a wise recognition of the need, at points, to accede to, rather than protest against, the demands of reality. As Lao Tzu puts it, to be wise is to have learnt how one must sometimes 'surrender to the whole universe'. Reason allows us to calculate when our wishes are in irrevocable conflict with reality, and then bids us to submit ourselves willingly, rather than angrily or bitterly, to necessities. We may be powerless to alter certain events but, for Lao Tzu, we remain free to choose our attitude towards them. It is in an unprotesting acceptance of what is truly necessary that we find the distinctive serenity and freedom characteristic of a Daoist.

Water as wisdom

IT MAY SOUND STRANGE to elevate something as ubiquitous as water to a philosophical element, but for Daoism, water is one of the central teachers of wisdom. It encapsulates, in ways we should study and be inspired by, the essence of Daoist thought, which is why so many Daoist temples and shrines are situated either near streams or have a fountain in their courtyards. The genius of water lies in its suppleness. It flows apparently effortlessly around obstacles and elegantly conforms to the existing contours of all things. Nevertheless, it is powerful enough – over time, and that is the key point – to wear away stone. We should try to become as water, says Lao Tzu. By contrast, too often, we try to change unpleasant things immediately, as if we were a battering ram, failing to reconcile ourselves to them, protesting hysterically and then losing our composure and strength. We do this particularly around unpleasant authority figures, tricky family members and administrative struggles. With Lao Tzu's example in mind, we should have some of the long-term ambition and deft patience of a stream wearing away at a block of granite.

Bamboo as wisdom

EAST ASIA HAS BEEN CALLED the Bamboo Civilisation, not merely because bamboo has been widely used in daily life, but also because its symbolic qualities have been described and celebrated for hundreds of years in the philosophy of Daoism. Bamboo is classified as a grass rather than a tree, yet it is tall and strong enough to create groves and forests. Unlike a tree trunk, the stems of bamboo are hollow, but its inner emptiness is a source of its vigour. It bends in storms, sometimes almost to the ground, but then springs back resiliently. We should, says Lao Tzu, 'become as bamboo is'. The greatest painter of bamboo was the Daoist poet, artist and philosopher Zheng Xie of the Qing Dynasty. Zheng Xie is said to have painted 800 pictures of bamboo forests, seeing in them a perfect model of how a wise person might behave. Beside one pen and ink drawing of bamboo, he wrote in elegant script: 'Hold fast to the mountain, take root in a broken-up bluff, grow stronger after tribulations, and withstand the buffeting wind from all directions.' It was a message addressed to bamboo but meant, of course, for all of us.

Kintsugi (JAPANESE):
Hope in brokenness

SINCE THE 16TH CENTURY, Zen Buddhist philosophy in Japan has been alive to the particular beauty and wisdom of things that have been repaired. *Kintsugi* is a compound of two ideas: *Kin* meaning 'golden', and *tsugi* meaning 'joinery'. In Zen aesthetics, the broken pieces of an accidentally smashed pot should never be tossed away; they should be carefully picked up, reassembled and then glued together with lacquer inflected with a luxuriant gold powder. There should be no attempt to disguise the damage; the point is to render the fault lines beautiful and strong. The precious veins of gold are there to emphasise that breaks have a rich merit all of their own. This is a profoundly poignant idea, because we are all in some way broken creatures. It is not shameful to need repair; a mended bowl is a symbol of hope that we too can be put together again and still be loved despite our evident flaws.

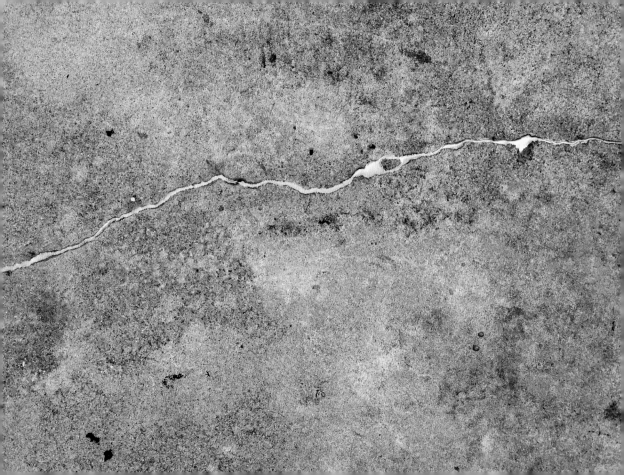

Wabi sabi (JAPANESE):
Loving the imperfect

IN *THE LETTER OF THE HEART*, written in Kyoto in 1488, the Japanese philosopher Murato Shuko laid out a distinctive new vision of beauty that merged two concepts: *wabi* meaning the bittersweet melancholy of being on one's own, and *sabi* the marks of aging and wear that can enhance an object. Shuko was translating into artistic and aesthetic terms a central principle of the Zen Buddhist ideal of wisdom: that we should embrace signs of time and evidence of imperfection, whether in objects, parts of the landscape, our houses, or ourselves. By loving and appreciating a simple rustic cup, an old roof tile, or a slightly messy scattering of leaves on a path, we are symbolically making peace with our transient, imperfect and unheroic natures. Flaws should not be artificially concealed; traces of damage should be allowed to remain evident. *Wabi sabi* invites us to a reconciliation with our true unvarnished human essence.

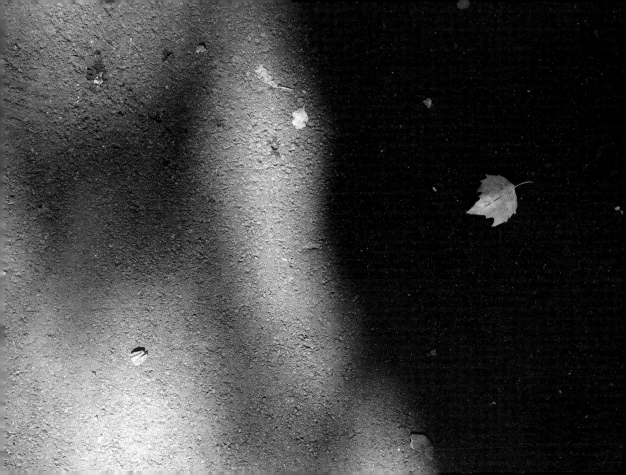

Gongshi (CHINESE):
Spirit stones

IN THE 9TH CENTURY, during the Tang Dynasty, an enthusiasm for rocks developed in Chinese philosophical culture based on the idea that rocks were at once very ordinary and very beautiful – and therefore a symbol of everything that we tend to overlook and should strive not to forget. The capacity to appreciate a stone indicated an enlightened mindset ready to identify value in unexpected places. As part of this petrophilia (love of rocks), poems were written to large, eroded and irregularly contoured rocks. Some philosophers called their rocks 'brother' or 'friend', and tourism developed around places where stones with especially interesting colours, textures and cracks could be found. It wasn't so much the rocks themselves that were important; what was being emphasised was the attitude of sensitivity, imagination and enchantment that might lead one to notice them. We might bring a comparably careful and generous gaze to bear upon many currently under-recognised sources of pleasure and consolation: clouds or rain, weeds growing at the side of the street, or a tender but not especially prestigious or beautiful friend.

Yinshi (CHINESE):
A recluse

MANY OF ASIA'S GREATEST PHILOSOPHERS have lived as recluses: on the side of a mountain, in a simple hut, without much money or fame, away from the bustle of cities. The choice has been honoured with a term, *yinshi*, which indicates not simply someone who lives quietly, but someone who is thereby inwardly enriched and enhanced. Away from others, we have a chance to reacquaint ourselves with our deeper thoughts and less socially compromised ways of thinking. Without a constant awareness of what other people consider normal, we're free to be creative and original. Traditionally, a reclusive life was associated with acquiring a small house deep in the countryside, yet in the 4th century, Tao Yuanming, a senior Chinese bureaucrat who had no chance to escape a pressured job, wrote a poem that began with the line: 'I built my hut in the midst of people'. One can (and frequently should) retreat into oneself even while lacking the option of fleeing the crowded city. We may not need an actual hut; just a version of a hut in our minds.

Ikebana (JAPANESE):
Flower arranging

AN ESPECIALLY CHARMING ASPECT of Zen Buddhism is that it recommends flower arranging as a prestigious philosophical discipline. In the art of *ikebana* one is asked to place flowers in a vase with enormous care, according to a dauntingly precise set of rules about their position, length and number. The real point is to spend time contemplating the sheer beauty of these modest bits of nature. It is hard to appreciate flowers when one is ambitious in a worldly sense and in a hurry for pleasure; flowers can seem humiliatingly small and inconsequential. But once we have lived a little and taken on board Buddhism's lessons about suffering, flowers may start to seem somewhat different: no longer a petty distraction from a mighty destiny, no longer an insult to ambition, but a genuine pleasure amid a litany of troubles; an invitation to bracket anxieties and keep self-criticism at bay; a small resting place for hope in a sea of disappointment.

Tea ceremony

HAVING A CUP OF TEA IN A RITUALISED WAY, reading poems and philosophical texts with friends in a tea hut in the garden while the water boils, is a central part of Zen Buddhist philosophy. The practice was created in the 16th century by the poet and thinker Sen no Rikyū. Properly performed, a tea ceremony was meant to promote what Rikyū termed *wa* or 'harmony', which would emerge as participants sipped their drinks and rediscovered their connections to their deeper selves, to nature and to one another. Then might come an emotion known as *kei* or 'sympathy', the fruit of sitting in a confined space with others, and being able to converse with them free of the pressures and artifices of the social world. A successful ceremony would leave its participants with a feeling of *jaku,* or 'tranquillity', a concept typical of Rikyū's calming philosophy. We learn from the ceremony that it is the true task of philosophy not just to formulate ideas, but also to work out mechanisms by which these may stick more firmly and viscerally in our minds.

Haiku

MANY OF WESTERN PHILOSOPHY'S GREATEST texts have run to hundreds of thousands of words. Some of the deepest works of Zen philosophy have been written in the form of three-line poems. Haikus, as these are known, contain three parts: two images and a concluding line that helps to juxtapose them. The best-known haiku in Japanese philosophy is called 'Old Pond', by Matsuo Bashō: *Old pond / A frog leaps in / Water's sound.* It is deceptively simple, yet, when one is in the right frame of mind, contains a gracious call to redemptive reverie. Here is another by Bashō: *Violets / how precious on / a mountain path.* Basho believed that poetry could ideally allow one to feel a brief sensation of merging with the natural world. Through language, one might become the rock, the water, the stars, leading to an enlightened and prized frame of mind known to Zen Buddhist philosophers as *muga*, or 'a loss-of-awareness-of-oneself'.

古池や蛙飛び込む水の音

ふるいけやかわずとびこむみずのおと

Gravel raking

THE ZEN BUDDHIST MONKS of medieval Japan recommended that, in order to achieve peace of mind, members of a monastery should regularly rake the gravel of their intricately plotted and bounded temple gardens around Kyoto. Within the confines of a large courtyard space, the monks could bring coherence and beauty to fruition. It wasn't easy. The monks loved to make ambitious patterns of swirls and circles. But it could – eventually – all be put right. The practice of raking gravel enshrines the Zen Buddhist idea that we can aim to make things perfect within a bounded space (a garden, a book, a home), but should gracefully accept the permanently chaotic nature of the wider world. Seeing a gravel garden can feel poignant because we recognise both the disciplined willpower that went into its creation, and sense the garden's fragility and impermanence, one sharp gust of wind away from being returned to chaos. It is the philosophy of Zen compacted into artfully raked lines.

Mono No Aware (JAPANESE): *The pathos of things*

THE PHRASE DESCRIBES an acute sensitivity to the short-lived nature of existence and, especially, of beautiful things. It indicates a melancholy awareness that everything we love and enjoy will fade, but rather than generating despair, this prompts a more intense and more poignant enjoyment of life's short-lived splendour. In Zen Buddhism, the sight of cherry blossom became a central object of this complex emotion; the full loveliness of the delicate flowers of the tree may last for only a few days, but it is all the more intense for this agonising brevity. Or the emotion might be evoked by the beauty of a cloud passing in front of a full moon at night, or a heron flying low across a misty lake in autumn. We should see these things as symbols of a fundamental Buddhist truth: our existence is also brief; we too will wither, fade and die. This is no cause for despair; merely grounds to keep the brevity of life clearly in view and to value our time all the more for the short opportunity we have been granted.

Shufa (CHINESE): *Calligraphy*

WESTERN PHILOSOPHY HAS NEVER paid particular attention to how its words have been represented on paper. For its part, Eastern philosophy has thought it vital for the success of its ideas that they be written elegantly by hand on large scrolls hung in living rooms and public spaces, according to the complex Chinese art of *shufa*. Philosophers might practise for years how to compose key sentences of Lao Tzu's *Tao Te Ching* or Confucius's *Analects*. The central piece of decoration in a room might be a scroll with just a single word on it, such as *ren* ('compassion': a cardinal concept in Confucian philosophy). Through contemplating beautiful pieces of calligraphic philosophy, it was hoped, the virtues they described might enter the soul of the beholder with special force. The viewer might acquire some of the qualities of the written characters themselves: uprightness, composure, flow. The implicit view is that it may not be enough just to be presented with a standard block of text; we may need to see characters formed by an unusually adroit human hand so as to make sure they stick in our fitful and erratic minds.

Published in 2020 by The School of Life
First published in the USA in 2021
70 Marchmont Street, London WC1N 1AB
Copyright © The School of Life 2020
Designed and typeset by Marcia Mihotich

Printed in China by Leo Paper Group

A proportion of this book has appeared online at
www.theschooloflife.com/thebookoflife

The School of Life is a resource for helping us
understand ourselves, for improving our relationships, our careers and our social lives –
as well as for helping us find calm and get more
out of our leisure hours. We do this through
creating films, workshops, books and gifts.

www.theschooloflife.com

ISBN 978-1-912891-47-4

10 9 8 7 6 5 4 3 2 1

The School of Life is a global organisation helping people lead more fulfilled lives. It is a resource for helping us understand ourselves, for improving our relationships, our careers and our social lives – as well as for helping us find calm and get more out of our leisure hours. We do this through films, workshops, books, gifts and community. You can find us online, in stores and in welcoming spaces around the globe.